RIDING THE WAVE OF TRUTH AND ACTION

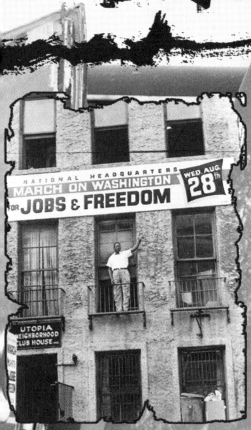

NATIONAL HEADQUARTERS
MARCH ON WASHINGTON
FOR **JOBS & FREEDOM**
WED. AUG. **28**th

UTOPIA
NEIGHBORHOOD
CLUB HOUSE INC.

GET ON BOARD

07   08   09   10   11   12   13   14   15   16—10   9   8   7   6   5   4   3   2   1

MANUFACTURED IN THE UNITED STATES OF AMERICA

Editorial Team
Editor: Josh Tinley
Production Editor: Pam Shepherd
Writers: Barb McCreight and Josh Tinley

Design Team
Design Manager: Keely Moore
Designer: Keely Moore

Cover Design by Keely Moore

Contents

Let us love, not in word or speech, but in truth and action.

—1 John 3:18

Day

Answer the Call

Memory Verse: "Obey my voice, and I will be your God, and you shall be my people." (Jeremiah 7:23)

In This Session

In a culture that celebrates the spirit of the individual, many people don't like to be told what to do. But we all need authorities in our lives who can guide us and help us make the right decisions. As Christians, we look to God for guidance and listen for God's voice. In this session, we look at what God is calling us to do and how we can answer God's call.

Time Traveling

Ancient Israel: God calls Gideon to lead the Israelites in battle against Midian. At first, the little guy from the tribe of Manasseh isn't sure he wants the job (see **Judges 6:11–7:21**).

The 1960's: The Peace Corps comes into being, giving young people a chance to answer the call to serve by spending two years living and working in a developing nation.

Today: When a tornado hits Hendersonville, Tennessee, the youth at Good Shepherd United Methodist Church answer God's call to help their neighbors.

Retro Object: Rotary Phone

Before telephones had touch pads with each number on its own button, they had rotary dials. These circular dials had ten holes—one hole for each numeral. A person dialed a rotary phone by putting his or her finger in the hole for the appropriate number, turning the dial clockwise as far as it would go, then releasing the dial. This process was repeated for each digit in the phone number a person was dialing. In the 1960's the first Touch-Tone phones were marketed, and over the next few decades, rotary phones were slowly phased out.

The rotary phone is the Retro Object for today because of this session's emphasis on answering God's call.

5

Judges 6:11-24: The Call of Gideon

Now the angel of the LORD came and sat under the oak at Ophrah, which belonged to Joash the Abiezrite, as his son Gideon was beating out wheat in the wine press, to hide it from the Midianites. The angel of the LORD appeared to him and said to him, "The LORD is with you, you mighty warrior." Gideon answered him, "But sir, if the LORD is with us, why then has all this happened to us? And where are all his wonderful deeds that our ancestors recounted to us, saying, 'Did not the LORD bring us up from Egypt?' But now the LORD has cast us off, and given us into the hand of Midian." Then the LORD turned to him and said, "Go in this might of yours and deliver Israel from the hand of Midian; I hereby commission you." He responded, "But sir, how can I deliver Israel? My clan is the weakest in Manasseh, and I am the least in my family." The LORD said to him, "But I will be with you, and you shall strike down the Midianites, every one of them." Then he said to him, "If now I have found favour with you, then show me a sign that it is you who speak with me. Do not depart from here until I come to you, and bring out my present, and set it before you." And he said, "I will stay until you return."

So Gideon went into his house and prepared a kid, and unleavened cakes from an ephah of flour; the meat he put in a basket, and the broth he put in a pot, and brought them to him under the oak and presented them. The angel of God said to him, "Take the meat and the unleavened cakes, and put them on this rock, and pour out the broth." And he did so. Then the angel of the LORD reached out the tip of the staff that was in his hand, and touched the meat and the unleavened cakes; and fire sprang up from the rock and consumed the meat and the unleavened cakes; and the angel of the LORD vanished from his sight. Then Gideon perceived that it was the angel of the LORD; and Gideon said, "Help me, Lord GOD! For I have seen the angel of the LORD face to face." But the LORD said to him, "Peace be to you; do not fear, you shall not die." Then Gideon built an altar there to the LORD, and called it, The LORD is peace. To this day it still stands at Ophrah, which belongs to the Abiezrites.

6

1960'S CULTURAL CONNECTION: THE PEACE CORPS

During a late-night campaign speech at the University of Michigan in October 1960, presidential candidate John F. Kennedy challenged students to give two years of their lives to help persons in developing nations. Months later, as the newly elected President of the United States, Kennedy signed an executive order officially establishing a program he called the "Peace Corps."

In the fall of 1961, the government commissioned the first group of Peace Corps volunteers, some of whom went to work in Ghana and some of whom headed for Tanzania. Within two years, there were over 7,000 Peace Corps volunteers working in 44 countries around the world. In the 47-year history of the program, more than 180,000 volunteers have answered the call, serving in 138 nations. Today, the nearly 8,000 active Peace Corps workers are focused on issues such as HIV/AIDS prevention and education and giving people in developing nations greater access to information technology.

President Kennedy famously said during his 1961 inaugural address, "Ask not what your country can do for you—ask what you can do for your country." Americans have always had the opportunity to serve their country by joining the military; the Peace Corps gave young people in the United States yet another way to answer Kennedy's call to serve. More recently, in 1993, AmeriCorps was formed. AmeriCorps is a network of thousands of organizations devoted to community service in the United States. AmeriCorps gives Americans a host of ways they can serve their country by working in their individual neighborhoods and cities.

7

CURRENT-DAY CONNECTION: "WHO ANSWERED THE CALL?"

On April 7, 2006, some members of the youth group at Good Shepherd United Methodist Church in Hendersonville, Tennessee, had gathered at the church to prepare for a concert they were to host that evening. But they decided to cancel the event because of the inclement weather.

While the youth were gathered, a tornado touched down nearby. When they emerged from the church building, where they had huddled for safety, the youth learned that the tornado had struck a house in a residential area near their church. A mother and two of her children had been rushed to Vanderbilt University Medical Center in nearby Nashville.

Upon learning that this family in their neighborhood had been hurt and lost their home, the Good Shepherd youth group decided to help in any way they could. As Christians, they knew that God had placed them in that situation to help neighbors in need. So once the bad weather passed, the teens went to where the house had stood and began cleaning up and salvaging the family's possessions. They stored what they were able to save at the church.

Because of the tornado damage in the community, many area schools were cancelled for the next few days. Instead of spending those days sleeping, watching television, hanging out with friends, or going to the mall, the youth at Good Shepherd used the time to continue the work they began after the tornado first hit. Youth minister Jennifer Mazzola referred to what her youth did as "living out Scripture," but she also emphasized that, as Christians, they were just doing what they were supposed to do.

8

Keep God's Commandments and Observe Them Diligently

While we believe that we are saved by grace through faith in Christ, the Bible tells us that we should respond to God's grace by obeying God's law. The Jewish people have identified and recognize 613 commandments in the Torah (first five books of the Bible) alone! Add to that number the teachings of Jesus and commandments found in the New Testament Epistles and you have a whole lot of rules to follow.

Let's start with the basics. Review the Ten Commandments (listed below and in **Exodus 20:1-17**). Which of these commandments is most difficult for you to obey? (You can interpret "adultery" to mean being unfaithful in any relationship, such as turning your back on a friend or breaking a promise to a parent. Likewise "making an idol" may include putting anything in your life—such as money or popularity—before God.) In the space below, write a prayer asking God to help you better obey this commandment.

- You shall have no other gods before me.
- You shall not make for yourself an idol.
- You shall not make wrongful use of the name of the LORD your God.
- Remember the sabbath day, and keep it holy.
- Honor your father and your mother.
- You shall not murder.
- You shall not commit adultery.
- You shall not steal.
- You shall not bear false witness against your neighbor.
- You shall not covet.

Day 2 Be Kind to Every Type

Memory Verse: "As God's chosen ones, holy and beloved, clothe yourselves with compassion, kindness, humility, meekness, and patience." (Colossians 3:12)

In This Session

Kindness is a virtue that we hear about a lot but that can be difficult to define. Being kind is more than just being nice. Kindness means being humble, unselfish, patient, sympathetic, and generous. This session looks at great ambassadors of kindness from different eras and equips youth with practical ways of showing kindness to their neighbors.

Time Traveling

<u>Ancient Israel:</u> David goes out of his way to show kindness to his friend Jonathan's son, Mephibosheth, even though Mephibosheth could be a potential political rival (see **2 Samuel 9:1-11**.)

<u>The 1960's:</u> Mother Teresa and the Missionaries of Charity show kindness to people throughout the world, particularly poor people suffering from leprosy in India.

<u>Today:</u> A group of young adults—The Simple Way community—move into a depressed Philadelphia neighborhood to extend kindness to their neighbors.

Retro Object: Manual Typewriter

Believe it or not, people were typing long before they had access to personal computers. The typewriter came of age in the late nineteenth and early twentieth centuries, and for much of the 1900's, the typewriter was the preferred way of transferring words onto paper in a neat, professional-looking manner. In the 1960's, IBM introduced its "Selectric Typewriters," which gave users a way to change fonts and to store and edit text before printing it on the page. Still, many people in the sixties were using the one-font, non-correcting, clickety-clack machines that now take up space in attics, basements, and museums.

The typewriter is the Retro Object for today because of this session's emphasis on God's command for us to show kindness to every *type* of person.

10

Second Samuel 9:1-11: David Shows Kindness to Mephibosheth

David asked, "Is there still anyone left of the house of Saul to whom I may show kindness for Jonathan's sake?" Now there was a servant of the house of Saul whose name was Ziba, and he was summoned to David. The king said to him, "Are you Ziba?" And he said, "At your service!" The king said, "Is there anyone remaining of the house of Saul to whom I may show the kindness of God?" Ziba said to the king, "There remains a son of Jonathan; he is crippled in his feet." The king said to him, "Where is he?" Ziba said to the king, "He is in the house of Machir son of Ammiel, at Lo-debar." Then King David sent and brought him from the house of Machir son of Ammiel, at Lo-debar. Mephibosheth son of Jonathan son of Saul came to David, and fell on his face and did obeisance. David said, "Mephibosheth!" He answered, "I am your servant." David said to him, "Do not be afraid, for I will show you kindness for the sake of your father Jonathan; I will restore to you all the land of your grandfather Saul, and you yourself shall eat at my table always." He did obeisance and said, "What is your servant, that you should look upon a dead dog such as I?"

Then the king summoned Saul's servant Ziba, and said to him, "All that belonged to Saul and to all his house I have given to your master's grandson. You and your sons and your servants shall till the land for him, and shall bring in the produce, so that your master's grandson may have food to eat; but your master's grandson Mephibosheth shall always eat at my table." Now Ziba had fifteen sons and twenty servants. Then Ziba said to the king, "According to all that my lord the king commands his servant, so your servant will do." Mephibosheth ate at David's table, like one of the king's sons.

Day 2: Be Kind to Every Type

1960's Cultural Connection: Mother Teresa and the Missionaries of Charity

The woman whom the world would come to know as Mother Teresa of Calcutta was born in 1910 in Skopje, which is now the capital of Macedonia. Her baptismal name was Gonxha Agnes, but she took the name Sister Teresa when she joined a Roman Catholic religious order known as the Sisters of Loreto in 1928. The following year she left for India, where she would spend much of the rest of her life.

Sister Teresa become Mother Teresa in 1937, when she made her Final Profession of Vows. In 1946, when she was working at St. Mary's School for Girls in Calcutta, India, Teresa received Jesus' call to establish a religious community that would serve the poorest of the poor. She went to work in Calcutta's slums and named her new Christian community the Missionaries of Charity. Teresa and her fellow nuns ministered to people dying from hunger, disease, and other effects of extreme poverty. She showed kindness and compassion to lepers at a time when there was no effective treatment for leprosy (also known today as Hansen's disease) and when fears that the disease was highly contagious led to many victims of leprosy being forced to live in leper colonies.

The Missionaries of Charity focused its efforts on Calcutta during the 1950's. Beginning in 1960, the Missionaries sent sisters into other cities and regions in India. The ministry continued growing throughout the 1960's. To empower men to meet the needs of India's poor, Teresa founded the Missionaries of Charity Brothers in 1963. In 1965 Pope Paul VI encouraged Teresa to start a similar community in Venezuela. Soon the Missionaries of Charity had a presence on every continent (except Antarctica).

Since the 1960's, the Missionaries of Charity has continued to grow, reaching more and more of the world's most vulnerable people. Mother Teresa was a leader in ministering to and providing services for orphans and persons who were dying, and she was a pioneer in reaching out to victims of HIV and AIDS. In 1979 she was awarded the Nobel Peace Prize.

CURRENT-DAY CULTURAL CONNECTION: THE SIMPLE WAY

In 1997 a group of Christian college students learned that a community of homeless people was being kicked out of an abandoned Catholic Church in Kensington, a poor neighborhood in North Philadelphia. Six of these students decided to buy and restore a house on Potter Street in Kensington and become fully a part of the neighborhood. The six housemates decided to name their community The Simple Way. (They also commonly refer to themselves as the Potter Street Community.)

Residents of the house work, eat, and pray together and with neighbors and guests. No member of the community is allowed to work more than a part-time job so that he or she can be ready to respond to needs that arise around the house. The residents are very intentional about sharing the workload so that no one has too much to do in the course of a week.

While the residents' relationships with one another are essential for The Simple Way, community members' relationships with their neighbors in Kensington are equally important. Members of the community have tutored and run art camps for neighborhood children and opened their doors to people who've needed a place to stay. In June 2007, a fire destroyed many homes in Kensington, including The Simple Way residence on Potter Street. Since then the Potter Street Community has organized work and raised donations to help the neighborhood recover. Potter Street resident Jean Schwartz says: "We have embraced this neighborhood and its culture as our own. We live below the poverty line. We are not heroes .... We are just six people living in a neighborhood, fighting for the rights of our neighbors, as well as ourselves."

The Simple Way shows kindness by recognizing the humanity and dignity of every person. Schwartz says: "Kindness plays a huge role in our community in so many ways, whether it's teaching the children on the block that fighting isn't the answer or the way that we talk to each other in the community. We have rules, such as no answering the door unless you can fully meet whatever need might arise on the other end (food, children wanting to play, emotional support, [or] just an ear to listen)."

Potter Street Community residents Robb and Zach take a break from chores to juggle some fruit.

Courtesy of The Simple Way

13

More Like . . .

A lot goes into being kind. Kindness involves being humble, unselfish, patient, sympathetic, and generous. Thus different people can teach us different things about how to be kind. What have you learned about kindness from the people described in this session and the people in your life? How can you become more like these people in positive ways? Complete the sentences below to discover ways that you can grow in kindness.

• I can be more like King David when he showed kindness to Mephibosheth by
_____

• I can be more like Mother Teresa and her Missionaries of Charity by
_____

• I can be more like the members of The Simple Way community by
_____

• _____ is a friend or peer who is almost always kind to others. I can be more like him or her by _____

• _____ is an adult whom I respect who is especially kind. I can be more like him or her by _____

We can learn much from the people around us and from the faithful people who came before us, and we can grow in faith by becoming like these people in certain ways. But there is one person whom we should strive to be like in *every* way: Jesus Christ. Throughout his ministry, Jesus taught us and showed us exactly what it means to be kind.

My Commitment to Be Kind: _____
_____

14

Day 3 · Clean the Record

Memory Verse: "And be kind to one another, tenderhearted, forgiving one another, as God in Christ has forgiven you." (Ephesians 4:32)

In This Session

Forgiveness was central to Jesus' ministry, so much so that after teaching the Lord's Prayer, he went back and emphasized the part about forgiveness. Today's Scripture is one of Jesus' most powerful illustrations of the importance of forgiving others as God has forgiven us. This session also lifts up some exemplary modern-day "forgivers."

Time Traveling

<u>First Century:</u> Jesus illustrates the importance of forgiving others as God has forgiven us by telling the parable of the unforgiving servant (see **Matthew 18:23-25**).

<u>The 1960's:</u> Leaders of the Civil Rights Movement are able to forgive (and ask others to forgive) those who senselessly and wrongfully murdered a young man named Jimmie Lee Jackson.

<u>Today:</u> Rick Walker is able to forgive the people who conspired to put him behind bars for a crime he did not commit.

Retro Object: 45 RPM Record

Before music was digital, people listened to music on vinyl records. Record players played these records at three speeds: 78, 33, and 45 revolutions per minute (RPM). 45 RPM records were usually seven inches in diameter and, since records were two-sided, often featured two songs. On one side was the popular hit song: the single. The other side—the "B-side"—usually featured a less-popular song. Though records were invented in the late nineteenth century, 45s debuted in the late 1940's. They sold consistently until the late 1980's, but peaked in popularity during the 1960's.

The 45 RPM record is today's Retro Object because this session emphasizes forgiveness, or "cleaning the record."

15

Matthew 18:23-35
The Parable of the Unforgiving Servant

"For this reason the kingdom of heaven may be compared to a king who wished to settle accounts with his slaves. When he began the reckoning, one who owed him ten thousand talents was brought to him; and, as he could not pay, his lord ordered him to be sold, together with his wife and children and all his possessions, and payment to be made. So the slave fell on his knees before him, saying, 'Have patience with me, and I will pay you everything.' And out of pity for him, the lord of that slave released him and forgave him the debt. But that same slave, as he went out, came upon one of his fellow slaves who owed him a hundred denarii; and seizing him by the throat, he said, 'Pay what you owe.' Then his fellow slave fell down and pleaded with him, 'Have patience with me, and I will pay you.' But he refused; then he went and threw him into prison until he would pay the debt. When his fellow slaves saw what had happened, they were greatly distressed, and they went and reported to their lord all that had taken place. Then his lord summoned him and said to him, 'You wicked slave! I forgave you all that debt because you pleaded with me. Should you not have had mercy on your fellow slave, as I had mercy on you?' And in anger his lord handed him over to be tortured until he would pay his entire debt. So my heavenly Father will also do to every one of you, if you do not forgive your brother or sister from your heart."

16

1960's Cultural Connection: The Civil Rights Movement

On the evening of February 18, 1965, hundreds of people streamed out of Zion Methodist Church in Marion, Alabama, and headed toward the city jail. They planned to protest the arrest and incarceration of a Civil Rights worker being held there. Though the jail was only a half block away from the church, a line of white city police officers, sheriffs' deputies, and state troopers stood between the largely black crowd and the prison. Suddenly someone turned off the streetlights. In the chaos that ensued, police attacked the protesters and the crowd scattered.

A group of police chased one group of demonstrators to a nearby café. According to an article in the *Anniston Star* (from Anniston, Alabama), "As the Troopers entered the café they immediately started overturning tables and hitting customers and marchers alike. In the melee, they clubbed 82-year-old Cager Lee to the floor and his daughter Viola Jackson when she rushed to his aid." Jimmie Lee Jackson, Viola's son and Cager's grandson, rushed to help his family. A trooper shot Jimmie in the stomach, and he died eight days later. He was 27. At least 10 other people at the café that night went to the hospital with serious injuries.

The same police who attacked the demonstrators on February 18 stood guard over Jimmie Lee Jackson's funeral. A group of hecklers was also present. Amid this hatred and animosity, Civil Rights leader Martin Luther King, Jr. spoke at Jackson's funeral. Writer Johann Christoph Arnold, who was present at the cemetery that day, recalls: "At the cemetery, King spoke about forgiveness and love. He pleaded with his people to pray for the police, to forgive the murderer, and to forgive those who were persecuting them."

Forgiveness born out of love was instrumental to the Civil Rights Movement and King's nonviolent philosophy. King wrote, "Love is the only force capable of transforming an enemy into a friend. We never get rid of an enemy by meeting hate with hate; we get rid of an enemy by getting rid of enmity. By its very nature, hate destroys and tears down; by its very nature, love creates and builds up."

King and other Civil Rights leaders wanted freedom and equality for African Americans; and they knew that, if they reached their goal, they'd have to learn to live peacefully with the people who'd oppressed them. Extending forgiveness to their persecutors was both a matter of faith and a matter of practicality. The goal of the Civil Rights Movement was not just equality; it was equality in a culture of peace, love, and justice.

While many Civil Rights leaders forgave their persecutors, they did not excuse these people's actions. Like Jesus, these leaders said: "I forgive you. Go and sin no more." (See, for example, **John 8:11**.) By continually speaking out against racism and injustice, while forgiving their oppressors, Civil Rights leaders transformed the hearts and minds of millions of Americans.

Current-Day Cultural Connection: Rick Walker

Rick Walker made some bad decisions in his life, but he was never a murderer. At age 30, Walker got mixed up in the drug culture of East Palo Alto, California. One night in 1991, Walker's ex-girlfriend died at the hands of a drug dealer to whom she owed money. The dealer, whose fingerprints were all over the crime scene, tried to cast off some of the blame by claiming that Walker had put him up to it. The prosecutor cut a deal with the drug dealer and another of Walker's former girlfriends to testify against Walker, and Walker was convicted as an accomplice to murder based on this testimony. His sentence was twenty-five years to life.

Instead of giving in to anger, Walker saw his wrongful conviction as an opportunity. He used his time in prison to overcome his drug addiction and turn his life around, becoming a lay preacher and counselor. He grew in his faith, and one aspect of his faith was learning to forgive those who'd wronged him. *San Francisco* magazine quoted Walker as saying, "There is nothing positive that can come out of me holding on to a grudge against a prosecutor or a judge.... Anger just hurts me."

Thanks to the efforts of Alison Tucher, a talented young lawyer whose mother served on the same school board as Walker's mother, Walker was released in 2003 after twelve years in prison. Following his release, Walker stayed true to his faith and maintained his message of forgiveness. Former San Francisco Mayor Willie Brown said of Walker: "He is the symbol of forgiveness. He is what all of us should try to be."

Forgiveness in the Real World

for•give 1. To excuse for a fault or an offense. **2.** To renounce anger or resentment against. **3.** To absolve from payment of (a debt, for example).

Complete the activity below, pausing to pray where the text indicates.

1. Read the definition above, then write your definition of *forgiveness*:

2. Name one person who has shown forgiveness to you:

3. Pray a one-minute prayer for this person.

4. Name one person you need to forgive: _____

5. Pray a one-minute prayer for this person.

6. What would it take for you to forgive this person?

7. Pray a one-minute prayer asking God for the strength to forgive this person.

8. Read the verse below.

> "[God] will again have compassion upon us; he will tread our iniquities under foot. [God] will cast all our sins into the depths of the sea."
>
> —Micah 7:19

9. Say a one-minute prayer thanking God for casting your sins into the depths of the sea.

19

Day 4

Act With Boldness

Memory Verse: "And this is the boldness we have in him, that if we ask anything according to his will, he hears us." (1 John 5:14)

In This Session

Boldness requires spunk and courage, but it also requires faith and conviction. Christ calls us to boldly act on what we believe in and to boldly confront injustice. Today we will meet people whose faith equipped them and inspired them to defy convention and act with boldness.

Time Traveling

First Century: The hemorrhaging woman boldly touches the fringe of Jesus' robe because she has faith that he can heal her (see **Luke 8:40-48**).

The 1960's: César Chávez and the Farm Workers Movement boldly demand better wages and working conditions for laborers in southwest America.

Today: Teenager Casey Robbins sleeps outside for an entire Minnesota winter to show solidarity with the homeless in her community.

Retro Object: Color TV

The color television isn't exactly retro since the average home has at least two of these "artifacts." But the color televisions of the 1960's were different from those in our homes today. There were no flat, plasma, or 50-inch screens; and cable television was just a way to transmit a few channels into homes that couldn't pick them up with an antenna. Sets popular in the sixties had 21-inch screens and were often encased in large, wooden cabinets. Viewers used dials, rather than buttons on a remote, to change channels. By the mid-1960's, the major networks were broadcasting several hours of color programming and sales of color TV sets soared. But color televisions would not outsell their black-and-white counterparts until the early 1970's.

The color TV is today's Retro Object because its bright, bold color enabled viewers to see things in new ways, and this session emphasizes boldness.

20

Luke 8:40-48

Now when Jesus returned, the crowd welcomed him, for they were all waiting for him. Just then there came a man named Jairus, a leader of the synagogue. He fell at Jesus' feet and begged him to come to his house, for he had an only daughter, about twelve years old, who was dying.

As he went, the crowds pressed in on him. Now there was a woman who had been suffering from hemorrhages for twelve years; and though she had spent all she had on physicians, no one could cure her. She came up behind him and touched the fringe of his clothes, and immediately her hemorrhage stopped. Then Jesus asked, "Who touched me?" When all denied it, Peter said, "Master, the crowds surround you and press in on you." But Jesus said, "Someone touched me; for I noticed that power had gone out from me." When the woman saw that she could not remain hidden, she came trembling; and falling down before him, she declared in the presence of all the people why she had touched him, and how she had been immediately healed. He said to her, "Daughter, your faith has made you well; go in peace."

21

1960's Cultural Connection: César Chávez and the Farm Workers Movement

César Chávez was born in 1927 in a small, adobe house in Arizona. Chávez became concerned with social justice when, as a small child, his family lost its home to a dishonest lawyer and investor. His upbringing was difficult. He attended thirty-seven different schools as a child, and he was unable to attend high school. Instead he educated himself by reading hundreds of books on various subjects. In 1942, when he graduated from the eighth grade, Chávez began working on a farm, picking lettuce and beets. A few years later, he founded his first labor union and began fighting for economic justice and better working conditions for farm workers, particularly those of Mexican descent who faced racial discrimination.

In 1962 Chávez helped found the National Farm Workers Association (NFWA). In 1965 a group of Filipino grape workers in Delano, California, who were members of the Agricultural Workers Organizing Committee, went on strike and asked Chávez and the NFWA to join the strike. The two organizations merged to become the United Farm Workers of America (UFW). Soon over two thousand workers had joined the Delano grape strike. The strike would last more than five years, during which Chávez led the striking workers in nonviolent tactics such as boycotts and demonstrations.

Under Chávez's leadership, the plight of farm workers—their poor pay and unsafe working conditions—gained national attention. In 1966 he led farm workers on a 340-mile march from Delano to the Sacramento capitol to pressure the state government to pass laws that would give the workers a right to negotiate collective bargaining agreements. Collective bargaining would provide workers a way to set terms and conditions for their wages and working conditions. The movement quickly spread, and during the sixties (and into the seventies and eighties), farm workers in the American west made tremendous gains.

When Chávez began his career as an organizer, he had limited education and scarce resources. But he accomplished extraordinary things through persistence and boldness. Chávez was a Christian whose activism was strongly grounded in his faith. One tactic he used was fasting. In 1968 Chávez underwent a twenty-five-day fast during which he ate nothing and drank only water. He described fasting as "a heartfelt prayer for purification and strengthening for all those who work beside me in the farm worker movement." His faith was also the source of his commitment to nonviolent resistance. The Farm Workers Movement never erupted in riots and didn't owe its success to high-paid lobbyists. Chávez and his fellow workers drew attention to their plight by marching, striking, and fasting.

Since Chávez's death in 1993, several cities have named streets, parks, and other landmarks after him. Today César Chávez's birthday—March 31—is a paid holiday for state employees in California. Texas, Arizona, New Mexico, and Colorado also recognize a César Chávez holiday.

22

Current-Day Cultural Connection:
Casey Robbins

Minnesota is notorious for being cold. And while being homeless is never fun, being without shelter is especially difficult when the temperature at night is consistently below freezing. In the fall of 2006, sixteen-year-old Casey Robbins of Hennepin United Methodist Church in downtown Minneapolis, decided to live in solidarity with the city's homeless population. Every evening from September 15 through Christmas Eve, 2005, Casey slept in a tent on the roof of her downtown Minneapolis home.

Casey's "100 Nights Outside" was more than just a sympathetic gesture. It was a campaign to raise awareness and to generate money for Dignity Center, a program at Hennepin United Methodist that helps persons in need of clothing, shelter, transportation, and other forms of assistance. Casey wrote about her experience and provided information about homelessness in Minnesota on a blog hosted on the church's website. Members of Casey's youth group joined her by also spending a night outside during the fall or winter. Casey's efforts caught the attention of local and national church leaders and challenged people to consider the plight of the homeless, particularly those living in unfriendly climates.

23

go forth with boldness

Jesus, after his resurrection, told the eleven disciples to "Go therefore and make disciples of all nations" (Matthew 28:19). "Making disciples" is also known as *evangelism,* a word that literally means "spreading the good news." Evangelism takes many forms—telling personal stories of faith, showing others how God is at work in the world, explaining what we believe as Christians, singing songs or creating works of art that point to God—all of which require boldness.

Answer the questions below to discover ways that you can boldly spread the good news of Christ:

1. Think of four or five people you know a little bit but would not consider as friends.

2. Would these four or five people identify you as a Christian? Why or why not?

3. If these people *would* identify you as a Christian, what could they learn about Christ from your example? If they *would not* identify you as a Christian, how could you express your faith more boldly?

4. How could you boldly show Christ's love to one or more of these people?

24

Day 5

Believe

Memory Verse: "Blessed are those who have not seen and yet have come to believe." (John 20:29b)

In This Session

Jesus famously told his doubtful disciple Thomas, "Have you believed because you have seen me? Blessed are those who have not seen and yet have come to believe." God gives us plenty of reasons to be believers: the stories in Scripture, the testimony of other Christians, and the magnificence of the world around us, among others. But ultimately, belief is an act of faith, made possible by God's incredible grace.

Time Traveling

First Century: Thomas is not willing to accept his fellow disciples' testimony that Jesus has risen unless he has physical evidence. Jesus is happy to oblige (see **John 20:24-29**).

The 1960's: The Jesus People emerge from the hippie movement and make believing in Jesus cool for a new generation.

Today: Teenager Tatyana McFadden believes in herself and inspires belief in others by becoming a world-class wheelchair athlete.

Retro Object: Box Camera

Although the first photograph was taken and developed in 1826, cameras were not widely available to the average person until the Kodak box camera was introduced in the late nineteenth century. Box cameras are very simple devices that capture images on film, but nothing else. (For instance, these cameras do not have a focusing system or allow photographers to change shutter speeds.) The first commercial box cameras were much larger than the cameras we use today and appeared to be brown or black boxes (hence the name). But by the 1960's, several smaller and sleeker box cameras—such as the Kodak Brownie 127, the Ansco Panda, and the Kodak Instamatic—made amateur photography more convenient and popular than ever. Box cameras are still sold today in the form of disposable cameras.

The box camera is today's Retro Object because cameras show us that there is more to reality than what we can capture on film and this session emphasizes belief.

25

John 20:24-29

But Thomas (who was called the Twin), one of the twelve, was not with them when Jesus came. So the other disciples told him, "We have seen the Lord." But he said to them, "Unless I see the mark of the nails in his hands, and put my finger in the mark of the nails and my hand in his side, I will not believe."

A week later his disciples were again in the house, and Thomas was with them. Although the doors were shut, Jesus came and stood among them and said, "Peace be with you." Then he said to Thomas, "Put your finger here and see my hands. Reach out your hand and put it in my side. Do not doubt but believe." Thomas answered him, "My Lord and my God!" Jesus said to him, "Have you believed because you have seen me? Blessed are those who have not seen and yet have come to believe."

Get on Board: Riding the Wave of Truth and Action

1960's Cultural Connection: The Jesus People

In 1967, during what was known as the "Summer of Love," a couple named Ted and Liz Wise formed a Christian community in rural Marin County in northern California called the House of Acts. That community would soon open a coffeehouse in San Francisco's Haight-Ashbury district. Haight-Ashbury was the heart of the hippie movement, and many hippies were attracted to what the Wises were doing. This community grew into a movement of free-spirited believers known as "Jesus People" or "Jesus Freaks."

In the years that followed, similar Christian communities, as well as Christian newspapers, popped up throughout North America. Hippie evangelists such as Lonnie Frisbee became minor celebrities. Baptisms in the Pacific Ocean were common. As musicians who joined the movement began writing rock and folk songs with gospel-inspired lyrics, contemporary Christian music was born. The movement also gave birth to organizations and denominations such as Calvary Chapel and the Vineyard Christian Fellowship. Duane Pederson, the founder of the *Hollywood Free Paper* (the unofficial voice of the movement), says, "I believed then, and still do, that the Movement began as the result of a spontaneous moving of the Holy Spirit."

The Jesus People aimed to emulate the early Christian community as presented in the Book of Acts. They believed in Christ, in the transforming work of the Holy Spirit, and in one another. Pederson recalls: "A Jesus house, coffeehouse, 'church in the park' or other outpost of the Movement in your city or town meant a place where you, and your dreams and fears and questions, were always welcome. A place that seemed light years away from the constant drumbeat of helicopters in Vietnam, light years away from the tear gas of protests on the campus quad. A place where you belonged and felt connected to something larger than yourself."

Photos from *The Hollywood Free Paper*, www.hollywoodfreepaper.org. Used with permission.

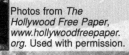

27

CURRENT-DAY CONNECTION: TATYANA MCFADDEN

Tatyana McFadden is one of the fastest wheelchair racers in the world. Though she was born with spina bifida, she doesn't consider herself disabled. In a February 2006 United Methodist News Service article, Tatyana is quoted saying, "When somebody writes 'disabilities,' they should cross out the 'dis' and just keep the 'ability,' because I think that everyone is able to do something."

Tatyana is able to do much more than something—she swims and plays ice hockey, basketball, and football—all without the use of her legs. When she was younger, she set world records for her age group in the javelin throw, swimming, and track.

Tatyana's belief in herself is grounded in the support of family and friends—including her church family at Linden-Linthicum United Methodist in Clarksville, Maryland—and her faith in God. And by her example, she's made believers out of others, including her kid sister Hannah, who lost a leg. Hannah says of her older sister, "She's been like the person who I look up to for all my problems." Tatyana has also passed on some of her basketball skills to Hannah and other children.

Tatyana won silver and bronze medals in the 2004 Paralympic Games in Athens, Greece, and hopes to compete in this year's Paralympic Games in Beijing.

28

The Apostles' Creed
(Ecumenical Version)

I believe in God, the Father Almighty,
    creator of heaven and earth.

I believe in Jesus Christ, his only Son, our Lord,
    who was conceived by the Holy Spirit,
    born of the Virgin Mary,
    suffered under Pontius Pilate,
    was crucified, died, and was buried;
    he descended to the dead.
    On the third day he rose again,
    he ascended into heaven,
    is seated at the right hand of the Father,
    and will come again to judge the living and the dead.

I believe in the Holy Spirit,
    the holy catholic** church,
    the communion of saints,
    the forgiveness of sins,
    the resurrection of the body
    and the life everlasting. Amen.

**universal

29

1960's Slang Dictionary

A GAS: fun, a good time

BAGGIES: loose-fitting swim trunks sometimes worn by surfers

BOGUS: not good, not true

BOOK: to leave one's current location ("Look at the time. I've gotta book!")

BOSS: good, cool ("Don't you think the Beach Boys are boss?"—from the 1973 movie *American Graffiti,* which is set in 1962.)

BREAD: money

CRASH: go to bed, turn in for the night

DECKED OUT: nicely dressed

DRAG: boring, no fun ("That dance last night was a drag.")

"GIMME SOME SKIN": "Let's shake hands"; "Give me a high five."

GNARLY: difficult, intimidating ("I've been surfing some gnarly waves this morning.")

GROOVY: cool, nice, good

"HANG LOOSE": "Chill out."

HANG TEN: to place all ten of one's toes over the front edge of a surfboard

JAZZED: excited ("I'm really jazzed about the new season of *Gilligan's Island*.")

"LAY IT ON ME": "Say what you need to say."

PAD: someone's house

PRIMO: exquisite

RAGS: clothes

RAUNCHY: gross, disgusting

SCARF: to eat a large amount of food in a small amount of time ("You really scarfed down that pizza.")

SHOTGUN: 1) the front passenger's seat of a car; 2) what one says to earn the privilege of sitting in the front passenger's seat of a car

SOLID: OK, acceptable

SPLIT: to leave one's current location, to book

TEACH: teacher ("I'll have my project done by Tuesday, teach.")

THREADS: clothes

WIPE OUT: to fall off one's board when surfing

31

Notes

Get on Board: Riding the Wave of Truth and Action